The Gospel According to

GOLF

Dr. Richard N. Ledford II

Heritage House

For Additional Product Information Visit:

www.MyRPT.org

Heritage House™
3881 North Monroe Street
Tallahassee, FL 32303

Manufactured in the United States of America.

Unless otherwise noted, all scripture references are from the
New King James Version of the Bible.

Scripture taken from The New King James Version © 1982 by
Thomas Nelson, Inc.

Cover design by Bill Johnson with Digg, Inc.

Library of Congress Cataloging-in-Publication Data
Ledford, Richard
Christian Living: 1. Golf. 2. Spirit Life. I. Title.

ISBN 0-9755579-0-4

10 9 8 7 6 5 4 3 2 1

First Edition

The Gospel According to Golf

Dr. Richard N. Ledford II

Introduction

Often times people have said to me, "Pastor, it seems that the gospel just doesn't seem relevant in our society and in our world today." I want to assure you, that is NOT true. The gospel is in fact very relevant to our modern society. I understand that in the fast paced world we live in that it has become easy to lose sight of the fundamental truths that God has laid out for us in the Word of God. We often get so caught up in the demands placed on us by everyday life that we are not able to see the simple correlations to the gospel that God has placed right in front of us.

In reality, God has made it simple for us to share His message of truth with the world. If we look carefully into our everyday activities we can find that there are definite connections that can be made to our modern lives and the gospel of Jesus Christ. In fact, if you carefully examine your surroundings, you can find God everywhere. His truths can be found in your job, going to the mall, in nature, and even on the golf course.

Golf, a sport of intrigue and precision, can not only provide endless hours of entertainment, but it can also provide life lessons that, if viewed with the right mindset, can lead you into a better understanding of God's fundamental truths. If you are a golfer, or you know someone who is, you can benefit from the lessons the game can teach you.

Throughout this book, I am going to take you on a journey through the game of golf and show you how it corresponds to the truths we find in God's Word. You will see that life is like a golf game in many ways; and if you will allow me, I will show you how to apply the principles of the game to your Christian walk, thus allowing you to become a knowledgeable and skilled player in the game of life. By applying the principles you will learn through the game of golf, you will gain an increased awareness of God's presence in your everyday activities.

Chapter 1
Finding Your Course

The Course Designer

The game of golf is a game of skill and strategy. In order to play with success you must first know your course. Your ability to strategize your club selection, swing motion, distance, and lie all determine your success of mastering the course. All these factors are first analyzed by the golf designer as he choreographs his outdoor design—the ultimate eighteen.

It is often revealing to know who designed a golf course. Certain designers are known for their unique features and styles. It may be their key positioning of sand traps, the size and elevation of the greens, the layout of the trees, and the location of the water that make the unique difference. When the course designers use their imaginations to their fullest they can make the best use of God's creation to make exceptional golf courses. A piece of nature is transformed into a place where people who love to play golf are challenged in their skills. The result is a symphony of beauty that surrounds the eighteen holes.

That symphony is made more beautiful by the realization that God has created all things—including us. God is the ultimate Designer of the course of life on which we play everyday. He has created us and everything on the earth as we know it. Any human golf course designer can only work within the boundaries of what God has already created. But God has no limitations when He works with us.

Knowing the Course

One of golf's finest pro championships is the Masters Invitational at Augusta, Georgia. Throughout Phil Mickelson's career he was plagued with poor shot selection and missed several opportunities to come out on top. Phil would drive well and get himself into position only to miss the green. He almost always elected to chip—or play a flop shot—using a 60-degree wedge. But the grain of the grass just off the greens at Augusta is such that Mickelson's wedge would stick rather than slide easily through the ball. As a result, Phil struggled year after year and found himself putting for double bogeys. But at the 2004 Masters, Mickelson made the proper adjustments. The grass at Augusta is always mowed so close on and around the greens, so Phil chose to use his putter instead of his wedge. This way he would have a chance for a par. It paid off, especially on the 18th hole.

Because Mickelson recognized his mistakes in the past at

the Masters he switched from his Scotty Cameron Futura putter to a classic blade putter. On the fast greens, Phil preferred the blade in order to feel the toe of the club releasing, or fanning back to square, on the forward stroke. Phil finally had a firm understanding how to play at Augusta. He is a prime example of a man who knew his course.

Reaching the Course

There is nothing like taking a ride on an early morning on the way to the golf course. I often gaze up to see the sky shimmering bright blue without even a trace of white brushed clouds. The air crisp and clean as the sun is shining softly down on the glistening green grass. Looking around I begin to examine the land before me. On my right stands a cluster of trees in a groomed wooded area and on my left is a large body of water decorated with a small area of beach sand. In front of me are the rolling green hills with a bright flag gently waving to me in the distance alerting me of my target. After a deep breath of the fresh fall air I can feel the comfort of a perfect 70 degree temperature pressing against my skin. Every thought of my day-to-day life diminishes and leaves me with only peace, relaxation, and focus. I turn, reach into my bag, pull out my driver, take a few practice swings, and feel my body rotate while conforming to the motion of my favorite club. A smile covers my face and joy fills my spirit as I realize that it is just God, the golf course, and me today.

God begins to speak to my heart and reveal to me how much this great game correlates with His gospel. As I stand there on the golf course I am reminded of the scripture in 2 Timothy 4:7, "I have fought a good fight, I have finished my course, I have kept the faith" (King James Version). Apostle Paul was telling Timothy that he had finished his race in life and that it was almost time for him to receive his reward from Jesus. If Paul had been playing golf, he may have said something like this: "Well, Timothy, I've taken my last stroke on the 18th hole. My match is over and now I'm going home."

It occurs to me that there are areas of the Christian life that can be compared to a golf course. For instance, when we are born we arrive on the earth with a purpose. As we mature in Christ that purpose becomes clearer and our focus narrows on the ultimate goal of our destiny. In order for us to arrive at the precise place that God has called us to, we must see the course, identify the obstacles, chart the journey and continue in the walk until we arrive at that final destination.

There are few people who begin a game of golf who do not finish it. Many of us have been tempted to throw our clubs down and walk away when the game was not going the way we planned. But there is always that driving force inside of us to finish the course, to continue until we reach that 18th hole, to take that last stroke, and to sink the putt. It may have taken a hundred strokes to get there, and there may have been some problems to deal with along the way, but we finish. It is not always easy to finish the course but the simple reward of completing the round brings more satisfaction than quitting a frustrating game half-way through.

I was playing golf with someone not long ago and he said to me, "You and Tiger Woods have a lot in common." I felt really good about that since Tiger is one of the best golfers in the world. My stance straightened and I stood tall. Then I asked him, "Really? What part of my game is it that you think identifies with Tiger's game? Is it that my drives are 300 yards down the middle or is it my tremendous short game and putting?" He said, "No. You're just like Tiger – you are in the woods all the time." Lucky for him, I had already put my club away!

During our journey to the destiny that God has called

us to, we will find along the course many things that will slow us down, stop us for a while, cause us to want to throw in the towel and walk away. But I assure you that if you hold on to the promise, if you keep the faith, then you will finish your game and you will feel a great sense of accomplishment in doing so. The course that life takes you down may have a few bumps, surprises and setbacks, but if you don't give up, you will see the reward at the end.

Chapter Two
Just the Right Setting

Quite often in our lives we may find it difficult to find even a moment to get away, be quiet, and listen to the voice of God speaking to our hearts. We are in our cars driving to our next appointment, talking on our cell phones planning our next three steps, rushing into work, sending e-mails and faxes to our colleagues to get business taken care of, only to find ourselves in a mad rush home to take care of our families, grab some dinner, and crash into bed for a few hours of rest before starting over again the next day. When do we have time to listen to what God might be trying to say to us? We are so busy, so rushed, and in such a hurry that even God sometimes has a difficult time getting a portion of our time.

Jesus said in John 16:33, "These things I have spoken to you, that in Me you may have peace. In the world you will have tribulation; but be of good cheer, I have overcome the world." God wants us to have peace in our lives. He wants us to be able to relax and enjoy the things He has provided for us in creation. He wants us to be still and focused enough to hear what He is saying to us. It was never God's intention for us to become so stressed out with the daily affairs of life that we cannot stop and enjoy Him and the things He has provided for us here in this life.

Many of the pastors I know play golf because it allows them to get away from the hustle and bustle of their daily lives. Golf was created to be a game of relaxation. The game is played in a very pastoral setting and requires quietness so that golfers can maintain their concentration and stay focused on the game without distractions. Since it requires a calm environment, it allows people to escape the rush and busyness of modern society.

There was a pastor who thought he deserved to take some time off since he had been very busy. He had a growing congregation and they were in the middle of a building project so he felt like he had every right to take a Sunday off and go relax. He needed to get away from the stressors in his life and take some time for himself to be refreshed and rejuvenated in his body. So early one Sunday morning he called his associate pastor, told him that he wasn't feeling well and that he needed him to fill the pulpit that morning because he was sick and needed to get some rest. The associate pastor was eager to help out so that the pastor could recuperate from his "illness." Free from his regular obligations, the pastor immediately changed into his golf attire, loaded his equipment into the car, drove to his favorite golf course, and began to play.

He stepped up to the first hole which was a 465-yard par 4. He hit the ball. Miraculously, the ball flew 465 yards and landed right in the hole. He was excited to have a hole-in-one and just knew that God was blessing him with a good game and some relaxation. He approached the second hole which was a 550-yard Par 5. He hit the ball as hard as he could and the ball soared through the air, just keeping to the edge of the trees. Incredibly, the ball flew 550 yards, an impossible feat for any mere mortal man. The ball bounced twice on the green and rolled right into the hole. He lifted his hands to heaven and yelled, "Oh God, THANK YOU!" The Lord looked down from heaven and said, "Enjoy it, because you will never be able to tell anybody about it."

Looking for Peace

God wants us to have peace in our lives. People often believe that it is not easy for us to maintain peace in our lives because of the modern age we live in today. But it is easier than most people think. In Isaiah 26:3 the Bible says, "You will keep him in perfect peace, Whose mind is stayed on You, Because he trusts in You." If we want peace in our lives, we need to stop worrying about everything around us and start trusting in God.

God is the only One who can handle all of the crises in our lives with the utmost perfection. If we trust Him to take care of all of the situations we encounter and we do not rely on our own strength or our own ability, then God will give us peace so we can relax in Him while He takes care of things. It seems that the more we become involved in trying to fix something or make it work out, the more messed up and confused the matter often becomes. That happens when we try and take care of things in our own way rather than allowing God to take care of them for us. He needs to be the One to show us what to do about every situation. He promises to keep in perfect peace all those who trust in Him. If we trust in God then we will have peace in our lives.

What is peace? Peace can be defined as an inner submission to God's will in one's life, a quietness of spirit that transcends human reasoning or authority. Peace is placing our hope and our trust in the One with whom we have been reconciled and allowing Him to have full reign in our lives. Peace is knowing, without hesitation, that whatever may come our way, God is on our side, since He wants the best for us. Whatever is happening, He will turn it around for our benefit. God knows what is best in our lives and if we can just trust Him, then He will work it out.

Golf is played on a course in a setting that provides surroundings conducive to quietness, concentration, and relaxation. If we make time in our lives and find a setting that provides these same qualities for us spiritually, then we will be positioned to hear more precise and direct instructions from God. In all actuality, God longs to talk to us and to share His heart and His plans with us. We only have to take the time to spend with Him so that He can pour these things into us. It can sometimes be difficult for us to take that time, but there is nothing more important in our lives than our relationship with Him.

If we neglected our relationships with people long enough, eventually we would drift away and lose contact with those people. They may even become more hesitant to share deep things with us and us with them. Why? Because trust diminishes when relationship is not constant. In order for us to maintain peace in our lives, we must do as Isaiah tells us: Trust in God. If we are spending time with Him and consistently cultivating that relationship, then we are able to hear Him speak to us, we know that He has our best interest at heart, and we deeply understand that He is in ultimate control. Therefore, we have no cause to not trust Him. However, if we have neglected our relationship and private time with Him, then we would doubt how involved He was in our lives since we could no longer sense His direction.

The bottom line is that God is no respecter of persons. Galatians 2:6 states, "…God shows personal favoritism to no man…" However, a person who gives his or her time to God and takes interest in Him will gain increased favor in his or her life. Proverbs 11:27 says, "He who earnestly seeks good finds favor…" Essentially, if God does something for one, then He is bound by His Word to do the same for another. But there has to be constant relationship with Him to set these things into motion. Relationship with God is the key to unlocking the door to limitless peace, trust, and favor.

I have to make time in my life each day and stop the craziness before it starts, then listen to what God is saying for my life, for my family, for the church I pastor, and for the community I live in. It is of the utmost importance that I am able to hear God's voice for direction in all of these areas. It is also important for each believer to spend intimate time with God every day. Each Christian needs divine guidance in order to live an exciting Spirit-led life.

Daily I look for a setting that is quiet and relaxing. This allows me to be able to focus on God and concentrate on the things that He has placed before me. In this resting place I hear His voice and am filled with peace. I am then able to trust Him. If you as a believer will make time each day to do the same, God's peace will also fill your life.

Chapter Three
Are You Wearing the Right Shoes?

Your Alignment

Sam Snead, an outstanding professional golfer from the 1930's, often practiced barefoot to gain a greater sensitivity for his weight distribution during his swing. He said that practicing barefoot forced him to swing with more consistency. Having the right balance begins with the right stance. He understood that the positioning of his feet could make or break his game.

In golf, your footing will control your balance. Your balance will be determined by your alignment. Alignment is two-fold. First you must position your body—especially your feet, hips, and shoulders—so that the spine aligns correctly. Secondly, you must stand in the correct location so that your ball will be in line with the target. When those two things are properly aligned, a good swing will more likely result in the ball heading in the direction of the target. If your back is misaligned, then your entire swing will be off which means your ball won't go in the direction you want. Or if you are facing the wrong way, if you are not aligned with your target, then you will also miss getting the ball to your desired location.

In our walk with God, alignment is also a key ingredient. It is the alignment of our hearts, our motives, and our actions that makes the difference. The more we focus on knowing and serving Christ out of a right spirit, the more likely it is that we will achieve His will for our lives. In golf, alignment is a shot-by-shot process. When we get off alignment, we need to take the time to recheck our position. Obstacles may come our way and confuse us and cause us get off the fairway and into the rough terrain. But if we continue to align our priorities and to keep our heavenly Father at the center of life we will engage in a long-life process of aligning ourselves with Christ.

A Firm Stance

A golf pro once told me that to have a powerful swing I must have a firm stance. The purpose of the firm stance is to get the most out of my swing. I learned that there are three sources of power where I get the most out of my swing: (1) body power, (2) arm power, and (3) wrist power.

It's helpful to have strength and muscle tone in the upper and lower body to hit the golf ball a great distance. More strength results in more power. If a golfer has more power he or she can use more lofted clubs, making it easier to hold the green.

Regardless of how powerful a person is, that strength must be properly harnessed and trained. It can be best put into practice through proper technique. The more a golfer swings the club correctly, the more powerful the arm muscles become. And over time the quicker that spark is generated from the club head to the hands.

Wrist power is achieved by the proper cocking of the wrists. Most teachers suggest that the wrists should be cocked after the body and shoulders have begun to turn. The wrists must be cocked so the club shaft remains on line with the target. If the wrists are properly cocked it has been said to account for 70 percent of the power in the golf swing. This is why small golfers are still able to hit the ball quite far. But those who combine all three effectively are the most powerful and accurate golfers on the course.

The analogy to spiritual life centers around the source of power. The power that we must have properly cocked or "loaded" is the power of the Holy Spirit. If we combine our talents, physical strengths, and mental focus with the prompting of the Holy Spirit, we increase our level on the playing field. We should not trust our flesh alone. We must receive the power available to us by keeping ourselves positioned in Him.

Having the right shoes is very important in the game of golf as well as in everyday life. If you start out on the wrong foot, or wearing the wrong shoes in this case, then you are sure to experience bodily pain and discomfort throughout the course of the day. If your feet are comfortable, then your entire body will be able to perform better. On the contrary, if your feet are uncomfortable, then your body will be uncomfortable and you will feel weak, lethargic, and may even experience pain.

The feet are the building blocks of the body. I know a woman who was born with a slight malformity in her feet. Without a trained eye, people would never notice it by looking at her. But recently she was told by her podiatrist that her feet were pronated. Her bones from hip, to knee, to ankle were at a slightly wrong angle. This meant that the area above the foot arch had too much pressure on it. This was causing the arches in her feet to become flatter along with other problems. She went to the doctor because she was having intense pain in her feet, back and neck. The podiatrist said she would likely develop knee and hip pain as well. So the physician instructed her to be very picky about what kind of shoes she would wear. If her feet could be correctly supported and kept comfortable, then the rest of the pain would diminish. She learned quickly that wearing the right shoes was of the utmost importance if she wanted to be able to carry out her daily duties with the most amount of comfort.

Shoes are certainly a critical piece of equipment when playing golf. Like any other sport, golf requires a special kind of shoe, often called spikes (metal, plastic, or spike-less). These shoes give proper support for the entire body and they also grab the ground allowing the golfer to maintain a firm steady stance.

What in the world do golf shoes have to do with the Word of God? In order to stand firm spiritually you must have the right stance. Your shoes are crucial to your stance. When you are in trying circumstances, you must have your feet shod with the gospel of peace. Ephesians 6:14-15 says, "Stand therefore, having girded your waist with truth, having put on the breastplate of righteousness, and having shod your feet with the preparation of the gospel of peace." When the enemy comes in and tries to bring circumstances your way that would cause you to fall down, he will not be victorious if you are standing firmly on the peace of God and trusting in Him.

> Blessed is the man who walks not in the counsel of the
> ungodly,
> Nor stands in the path of sinners,
> Nor sits in the seat of the scornful;

But his delight is in the law of the Lord,
And in His law he meditates day and night.
He shall be like a tree
Planted by the rivers of water,
That brings forth its fruit in its season,
Whose leaf also shall not wither;
And whatever he does shall prosper.
The ungodly are not so,
But are like the chaff which the wind drives away.
Therefore the ungodly shall not stand in the judgment,
Nor sinners in the congregation of the righteous.
For the LORD knows the way of the righteous,
But the way of the ungodly shall perish.

Psalm 1:1-6

If your feet are planted firmly in Jesus Christ as your foundation for truth, then the obstacles on the course of life won't deter you from your goal of finishing your match successfully. On the other hand, if you are watching the people behind you while you are trying to go forward, your body alignment, your footing, and your aim will be way off course. And then when your ball goes off the fairway and you end up in rough circumstances, you may tumble and fall.

In order to navigate effectively as a Christian through all the rough terrain, you must have the firm footing that comes only from having the gospel of peace firmly fitted on your feet. Wearing the right shoes can help you gain traction on otherwise slippery landscape. The enemy would like nothing more than for you to be trying to move forward in the things God has for your life but you not be able to arrive at your planned destination because you don't have the spiritual traction you need in order to cross the sometimes rocky, rough, or sandy geography.

The traction we gain from wearing the right shoes will not come from our strength, but from the power of God. He gives us what we need to overcome every obstacle the enemy tries to place in our path. Psalm 18 describes it like this:

> For who is God, except the Lord?
> And who is a rock, except our God?
> It is God who arms me with strength, and makes my
>   way perfect.
> He makes my feet like the feet of deer,
> And sets me on my high places.
> He teaches my hands to make war,
> So that my arms can bend a bow of bronze.
> You have also given me the shield of Your salvation;
> Your right hand has held me up,
> Your gentleness has made me great.
> You enlarged my path under me,
> So my feet did not slip.

Psalm 18:31-36

When God makes your feet like the feet of a deer, you can be sure your traction will help you navigate every possible kind of topography. Unlike the feet of an animal with single hooves or soft paw pads, the deer has a split hoof which gives it both the agility and endurance that a hoof can provide and the mobility and traction that a soft pad can provide. The outside edge of the deer hoof is hard allowing the animal to run and move smoothly over hard rocky terrain. The hoof is split so that when the deer is on soft, muddy terrain it can open. On the inner side of the hard hoof is a soft fleshy area with dewclaws. Dewclaws grab into the terrain allowing the deer to maintain traction in softer more challenging areas. Therefore, a deer can move much faster and more easily over multiple styles of ground than other animals would be able to.

It is also amazing that a deer can actually run faster on hilly, mountainous terrain than most of its enemies. This is because the hard surface of the hoof protects the soft area from injury from sharp rocks during climbing. It seems as though God actually created the feet of a deer to climb. That is why the psalmist said that having feet like a deer would allow him to travel "on high places."

So, when the enemy places a mountain in front of you, call on God and trust Him to provide you with the proper footwear for the course you are running. Just like golf requires spikes to provide a steady stance on the grassy course, your spiritual feet require the footwear only God can provide. When He makes your feet like the feet of a deer though the gospel of peace, you will be able to climb any mountain that the enemy places in your path with swiftness and grace.

Chapter 4
Playing the Game

Competition

Golf is a game that can stretch the greatest of athletes. It is where the playing ground becomes level. You might be at your best and unbeatable one day and humbled the next. For example, Tiger Woods finished in a tie for 22nd at the 2004 Augusta Masters Tournament. And at the same time, at the 2004 Sony Open, Michelle Wie, the 14-year old phenomena, birdied two of the final three holes on a 7,060-yard layout to beat 47 PGA Tour pros and come within an inch of continuing on in the tournament. The game has the potential to bring out the champion in you.

Typically when a person thinks about playing a game, any game, the first thing that comes to mind is competition. Nearly every sport requires a person to compete against someone else in order to obtain the satisfaction that comes from seeking and reaching a point of recognition in accomplishments in the chosen area of play. Golf is designed unlike a lot of other sports in that one person does not *have* to compete against other people. Golf can be played alone: one golfer against the course.

Each golf course is rated with a number for par, par 72 for example. That number means that the score you should aim for while playing on that course is 72. Each time you swing at or hit the ball, it counts as a stroke. In order to play a golf course that is par 72 the person playing would need to hit the ball no more than 72 times in 18 holes. This game is not about how well you play against your friend, but rather it is about how well you play against the course.

Children are taught from a very early age to compete for the attention of their parents or to compete for the best grades or the most friends in school. Even adults compete in all areas of life from climbing the corporate ladder, to having the newest gadgets, to owning the most expensive automobile, or to having the largest home. But this is childish. Each person should try to be the best that he or she can be with what that person has. The game of life is no different than golf. Life is not about how well you are playing against your friends, but how well you are playing your game against the odds.

Staying Focused

Being mentally prepared for life is the key to succeeding when pressure comes. On the 18th hole at the 2001 U.S. Open,

Stewart Cink had to hole his 15-foot putt to have any chance of beating Mark Brooks and tieing Retief Goosen, whose ball was just 12 feet away for birdie. Cink narrowly missed his par attempt and naturally he felt letdown. When he stepped up to make an 18 inch putt—a putt he would normally make 100 times out of 100—he rushed and then missed it. Now Retief Goosen had more room for error. He only needed two putts from 12 feet to win. But Goosen disastrously whacked his first putt two feet past the hole. Then instead of taking his time setting up for his last stroke, he choked. The two-foot shot missed badly and kept rolling past the hole. Goosen was tired from the heat, humidity, and 71 holes of nerve-racking championship golf. Now he was facing a three-foot putt for bogey and a chance to get into a playoff. I can remember the disgust on his face and how angry he looked when he finished the hole. He made the putt and went on to beat Mark Brooks in a playoff the next day.

Cink had no idea that Goosen would three putt. In the scheme of things, if Cink had made his 18-incher, he too would have been in the playoff with Mark Brooks. It was not a long putt but an 18-incher that cost him a chance at the championship. In life it is not always the big things that discourage us, it is the small things. The Bible says that the little foxes are the ones that spoil the vine (Song of Solomon 2:15).

Being focused is a key in golf. But it, too, must be balanced. You have probably seen people playing golf who stood over the ball for an exceptionally long time. They seem frozen in a trace. They stare at the ball while shifting their feet and waggling the club hoping to hit the best shot of their life. This standing over the ball for a long time occurs because many golfers think they need to ponder each shot. Thinking that they are focusing, they usually have no idea how much time they are wasting prior to each shot. Often the results are poor. Thinking about a shot should occur primarily before they stepped up to the ball. They should have a very brief, relaxed, and smooth pre-shot routine. But instead they can overdo it and drive the ball into the woods or out of bounds.

This brings us to the importance of having a good pre-shot routine even at the very highest skill levels. For example, in the 1996 Masters, Greg Norman's pre-shot routine for the first three days lasted an average of twenty-six seconds. At the end of those three days he led the tournament by a margin of ten strokes. On the final day, when Nick Faldo overcame that lead to win the tournament, Greg's pre-shot routine had risen to an average of thirty-eight seconds. Perhaps even Greg Norman was less at ease and therefore thinking too much during the final round. Being at ease is not always simple. Whether in our golf swing or in the challenges of life, it is easier to suggest being at ease than to do it.

God has given each man, woman and child a race to run during the course of his or her lifetime. One person's race may be worldwide evangelism, another person's may be local church leadership, another's may be success in the corporate market, and still another's may be success in child rearing. Whatever your particular race may be, the important thing is that you run your race and complete the task that God has placed before you. You will find the most success, the most favor, the most personal growth, and the most happiness in your life when you stop comparing your race to your neighbors and start accepting and doing what God has called you to do.

There is so much competition in the world that people often spend a lifetime trying to find success in a venue that they were never intended to walk in. Sadly, what often drives a person to this is the desire to look important in the eyes of others. People often think that in order to gain acceptance or admiration from others, they must be just like or better than the person they most admire. Worse than that is when people believe that they have to be like the person someone else admires. We all have a race of faith that we have to run and God is not comparing us to others and how well they are doing. God is only looking at where we are in relationship to our skill level and the toughness of our course. The first step is to be on the right course in life. I believe the writer of Hebrews says it best:

> Therefore we also, since we are surrounded by so great a cloud of witnesses, let us lay aside every weight, and the sin which so easily ensnares us, and let us run with endurance the race that is set before us, looking unto Jesus, the author and finisher of our faith, who for the joy that was set before Him endured the cross, despising the shame and has sat down at the right hand of the throne of God.
>
> Hebrews 12:1-2

It is a very dangerous thing to compare yourself to other people. This can cause an array of emotions to filter into your spirit and weigh you down. The only way to run your race and not compare yourself to others is to keep the focus of your faith on Jesus. He is the One who started and finished the race already; He is the one who has received His reward and is now seated in heaven in the place of honor. In order for you to finish your race and receive your reward, you must not look at what others are doing, but find where you are, focus on Jesus and move toward the goal He has given you. In simple words—mind your own business!

In the world we live in, competition surrounds us on every avenue. This mindset tends to stay with us throughout most of our lives. But we must reach a point where we realize that the most important accomplishments in life are usually not those obtained through competition, but those obtained by just living and being ourselves in all we do. God never intended for us to go through life competing with each other and trying to outdo the person who is already a step or more ahead of us. God's intention and ideal desire for us is to walk our own walk and live our own lives to the fullest potential that He has created us for.

So, in order to find satisfaction in your mind, body, and spirit, you should run your race and not worry about those around you. Let God guide you down the path of life that He has chosen for you. It is not how well you beat someone else on their path, but how well you walk out your own. Walk your own path and stay off of everyone else's and I assure you that you will receive the reward that your heart truly desires – the reward of an imperishable crown.

Chapter 5
Help Me, I Have a Handicap!

Golf is the most equitable game. It is a game for everyone despite a person's level of skill. Through the use of what is called a *handicap* the chances of equal competition are equalized. The game of golf takes into consideration that not everyone playing the course is going to easily obtain par. As mentioned before, par is the suggested number of strokes for a hole or for the course in perfect play. A handicap allows additional strokes to those who are less precocious in their play of the game. For example, if the course is a par 72 and you average 72 strokes in 18 holes, then you would have a zero handicap. However, if you are like me and you hit a lot more than 72 times when you play, you receive an allotted handicap. In other words, if my average game was usually an 85, then my handicap would be 13.

So how does my handicap of 13 make me equal to the person with a handicap of zero? If I were to play a game of golf with Tiger Woods, I would have an additional 13 strokes to my score. Therefore, in order for Tiger to beat my score of 85 he would have to shoot 71 or better. The handicap becomes extremely advantageous to the person who is able to utilize it.

There is only one small problem with having a handicap. In order for your handicap to benefit you the most, you have to be strong and secure enough to admit that you have one. In addition, when you do admit your handicap, you must be honest. When you are asked, "What is your average?"—for you to receive the most benefit to your game—you need an accurate average in order to figure out the correct handicap. In other words, to use a handicap you must be willing to admit that you are not perfect. It is our human nature that prevents us from being honest and confessing our shortcomings. There is no room for pride!

For a lot of people, it is difficult to admit that they have a weakness. Some are not as good as they would like everyone to think they are. I have been on the golf course with men who get all fidgety, nervous, and sweaty palms when they are asked what their handicap is. They shift from side to side and unconvincingly convey that they have a lower handicap attempting to show off their skill. The lower the handicap, the better a person claims to be. Here's the problem: when it comes time to perform, the truth comes out and everyone is able to see the illegitimate claim. If you say you have a handicap of 5 and you get out on the course and it takes 6 swings for your ball to leave the tee box, you have fooled no one but yourself. Everyone knows that you are a liar! So don't let pride stand in your way, just admit it—you have a handicap.

Overcoming Pride and Gaining Humility

Dealing with pride in our daily lives is no different. In order to receive the full benefit God has to offer we must be able to overcome our egos, admit that we have weaknesses, and recognize our limitations. The Apostle Peter tells us to be "'...clothed with humility, for God resists the proud, but gives grace to the humble'" (I Peter 5:5). In order to be a recipient of God's grace we must first be humble in His sight. Now humility is not to be confused with low self-esteem, lack of confidence, or the "poor me" syndrome. Humility is being confident about our strengths without arrogance and being honest about our weaknesses without insecurity.

When we are able to humble ourselves, then we will be positioned to receive the benefit of living a confident life. Apostle Peter goes on to say: "Therefore humble yourselves under the mighty hand of God, that He may exalt you in due time, casting all your cares on Him, for He cares for you" (I Peter 5:6-7). It may take humility on our part to admit areas of weakness, but the attributes and benefits gained will outweigh the results of lying to protect our pride. Our character is developed when we are honest with ourselves, honest with God, and honest with others. Honesty may sometimes cause temporary setbacks in the perception of others, but it will never cause a setback in the eyes of God.

Humility and honesty go hand in hand. They are two of the most admirable attributes of a person's character. When we are able to be honest before God then He is able to perform in us what is needed. He can provide His strength in the midst of our weakness. We can trust Him to lift us up to a new level in character, skill, and status.

Receiving His Grace

Humility ushers grace into our lives, whereas pride brings opposition from God. If we are humble and we receive His grace then we can be sure that we will have the necessary strength to overcome any obstacle in our path.

> And He said to me, "My grace is sufficient for you, for My strength is made perfect in weakness." Therefore most gladly I will rather boast in my infirmities, that the power of Christ may rest upon me. Therefore I take pleasure in infirmities, in reproaches, in needs, in perse-

cutions, in distresses, for Christ's sake. For when I am weak, then I am strong.

II Corinthians 12:9-10

The key to overcoming the obstacles in our lives is admitting our weaknesses and trusting the grace of God to provide everything we need to successfully complete the course we have each been given in life.

We all have weaknesses. We each have areas in our lives that others do not consider perfect. But God sees our weaknesses as an opportunity for us to lean on Him and then to overcome. He sees a doorway in our lives to enter into and a way to show Himself strong. Our areas of weakness are not areas that we should want to hide or be ashamed of. Paul said that he took pleasure in these things knowing that in Christ, he would be made strong. If we try to conceal the weaknesses that come from infirmities, needs, or distresses in our lives, then Jesus cannot step in and provide His strength we need. If we conceal the truth we will remain weak; but as we confess the truth we will gain His strength.

We need to be 100% honest with ourselves and with God. Without honesty, the gateway to grace is blocked by a lack of humility. Where there is a lack of humility there is evidence of pride, which brings opposition from God rather than grace. There is no truth in hiding or concealing the weak areas of your life. Jesus said, "And you shall know the truth and the truth shall make you free" (John 8:32).

So the first step to gaining the strength you need is to be honest, be humble, and admit your weakness. In doing this, you gain the needed strength from Him which makes your playing field of life equal with everyone else's. Regardless if it is with golf or in your life—it is not a matter of who is able to play the game with the least strokes or the least amount of weaknesses. It is about who is able to use all of the available resources to their fullest potential for the greatest benefit. Having a handicap is not a weakness; it is essentially a tool that makes your game equal with others. If you are playing your course, admitting your handicap, and receiving the benefit of the extra strokes, then you will find that your game has every bit the potential of being just as successful as the game of the person who has no handicap. Jesus has provided everything you need to have an equal playing field.

What we need to realize in our Christian experience is that having a weakness is not anything to be ashamed of. Admitting our areas of struggle can actually become a sign of strength, confidence, and character. In the long run, we are better off be-

41

ing honest about our weaknesses rather than dishonest about our "would-be" strengths.

I want to encourage you today to push aside your human nature and the desire to conceal the things you struggle with, admit them to God, and ask Him to make Himself strong in those areas of your life. I guarantee that if you do this, He will show up and prove Himself on your behalf, thereby providing a testimony of unequaled proportions. God has an amazing way of turning your weaknesses into stepping-stones. If you will just say, "Lord, I need help in this area," or "I'm battling in this area," then God will show up and provide for you a handicap to give you the extra help so that you can compete with the best!

Chapter 6
Watch Out for the Hazards!

Standing at a tee and staring at the ball the professional golfer begins to take his practice swing before taking his best shot. His goal is to keep it in the fairway. The onlookers realize that getting that little white ball into the hole several hundred yards away may not be as simple as taking a few swings. Not every shot will be straight. Shouts of joy do not follow every drive. Because between the ball and the hole there may be water, sand etched out as a piece of art, a wooded area, or a high grassy rough. These are the obstacles between the tee and the hole. They are called *hazards*.

The idea behind playing a great game of golf is to avoid the hazards. The goal is to keep the ball in the middle of the green as much as possible. This can sometimes prove to be easier said then done. I have an 85-year-old uncle who plays 18 holes of golf everyday. He cannot hit the ball very far with each swing, but he consistently hits the ball down the middle of the green. I may be able to hit the ball greater distances, but so many times my ball is off in the woods, landing in the water, or off in the sand. You can bet when I play golf if there is anything between the hole and me, my ball will find it!

Just like there are hazards in the game of golf, there are also hazards in life. The only way to stay out of the hazards is to stay in the middle of the road and avoid the ditches. Jesus said: "In the world you will have tribulation; but be of good cheer, I have overcome the world" (John 16:33b). Jesus has already defeated the hazards that we will have to face in life, so if we keep our focus on Him, then we too will be able to avoid the hazards and stay in the middle of our road.

What Are You Looking At?

Golf is not a purely physical game, but rather a mental one. The way the majority of golfers play successfully without succumbing to the hazards surrounding them on the course is to focus on the middle of the green. Many of them ignore the hazards and play the game as if they were not even there.

Through years of experience I have learned that our Christian walk is the same—it is not physical—it is mental. We are challenged to keep our minds in tune with the Word of God. The biggest battlefield in our spiritual walk is not on the outside, but inside the mind. The Bible says:

For though we walk in the flesh, we do not war

according to the flesh. For the weapons of our warfare are not carnal but mighty in God for pulling down strongholds, casting down arguments and every high thing that exalts itself against the knowledge of God, bringing every thought into captivity to the obedience of Christ.

II Corinthians 10:3-5

The enemy is a cunning character who avidly seeks to destroy every Christian. He will continually place distractions, traps, and spiritual hazards in our way hoping we will stumble or get caught up in one of the traps. The best option is to avoid the traps all together by being aware of their presence, yet not entertaining the possibility of being ensnared by one of them. Successful golfers know the hazards are present on the course, but in order to reach their goal, they must overlook the hazards and focus on the flag at the end of the hole more than on the hazards.

Christians can become ensnared by the wiles of the enemy because they focus too much on the surrounding hazards and not enough on the prize: "Not that I have already attained, or am already perfected; but I press on ... reaching forward ... I press toward the goal for the prize..." (Philippians 3:12-14). Disconsolate Christians often fall into the traps because they have

45

lost sight of the goal. But all Christians, in order for us to reach the mark set before us, must be aware of the schemes the enemy would desire to use to entrap us. We must not be overburdened by their presence. The more attention we pay to the hazards in life the larger they become. I'm sure you've heard the saying, "Don't make a mountain out of a mole hill." That is exactly what some people do when they focus on the hazards more than the goal. The longer we look at something the bigger and more impossible it becomes to conquer.

Jesus never intended for our journey to include every side tour through the hazards. However, the truth of the matter is that oftentimes we do fall into those traps and sometimes it can be very difficult to get out of them once we are caught. The only way to get our ball out of the sand trap in a game of golf is to dig our shoes into the sand gaining a steady stance, position ourselves over the ball, and swing behind the ball to loft it into position for the next shot. The key to the sand shot is to not hit the ball but to hit behind it. Use the sand to get under and behind the ball so that the ball can get the lift needed to get out of the bunker.

Likewise, when you find yourself in the sand trap of life, you must use your struggles to move your forward. Your trials and tribulations are intended to make you greater. At one time or another everyone finds himself or herself in a trap. Regardless of how you and I get there we need to see that what got us there can also get us out. Our hardships can either make us bitter or better. We will not get out by trying to hit the ball or by swinging too hard. We must allow the sand to act as a buffer and it will push us out. We must trust God that in the middle of our circumstances what is surrounding us can be used to get us out. Getting the ball back on course is what is important.

Stay in Bounds

One of the keys to a successful game of golf is to stay in bounds. If your ball goes off of the course (and mine does a lot) then you are considered to be out of bounds. If that happens it is a penalty and adds one stroke to your score. God has a course for our lives. Now ideally we are to stay on that course and not allow our lives to get carried away from the path he has directed us to walk.

How does a well-meaning Christian get out of bounds? Surprisingly enough, what often times gets a person off course are the things we don't think much about: telling a "white lie," spreading gossip, or going places we should not go. Other times, it may be the more obvious: jealousy, disobedience, fornication, theft, or adultery. Whether we engage in those seemingly meaningless sins or the more obvious ones, we will consistently suffer the consequences of those avocations. Hopefully we learn to steer clear of them in the future. Those sins may cost us friendships, reputation, strength, effort, money, or other resources. But in the end, we must focus on getting back on the green so that we can fully and completely finish the course.

Based upon examples in scripture, we should always weigh the consequences of our actions before making the decision to do things that would be considered out of bounds. Think of Moses—his disobedience cost him the joy of entering into the land of promise. Samson's disobedience cost him his anointing. David's adultery and act of murder cost him the life of his son and bloodshed in his own home. Solomon's failure to remain true and monogamous to God caused his kingdom to be split. The most important question we can ask ourselves is this: "What am I willing to sacrifice now to have the promises of God in my future?" Let's face it; sometimes the instant pleasures are not worth the enduring consequences in our lives.

The Small Things Count the Most
John Daly is considered one of the greatest golfers in

the world. He can hit a ball farther than anybody else. John can knock a ball 350 yards down the green. But golf is not always about how far you can hit the ball. Golf is also about a person's skill in the short game as well. There are a lot of people who are trying to catapult their lives forward by hitting the ball a mile. They may be trying to get into the ministry, gain a million dollars, win the game of life and win big. If a golfer's goal is to get his or her ball in the hole from 495 yards with one hit, that person will be constantly disappointed. But if the golfer focuses on keeping the ball on the fairway, getting it onto the green, and then putting it into the hole, that person will surely see success. An important thing to remember is that you don't win the game by having big swings all of the time, but by consistently getting the little swings right.

Again, your spiritual life is no different. Whatever your expectation may be in life, you will get there not by doing the big things right some of the time, but by doing the little things right all of the time. Remember my 85-year-old uncle? He didn't hit the ball far, but he kept it down the middle. If we are consistent in the small things we will stay in the middle of the course, then we will win the game in the long run.

Chapter 7
Get Yourself a Caddy

A *caddy* is a skilled attendant who carries a golfer's clubs. This person is extremely familiar with the courses played and with the golfer's ability. This allows the caddy to assist or suggest the right club for each swing. Traditionally, caddies were a central part of the golfing experience. However, as society has advanced and mechanical golf carts have become easily available the cart quickly replaced the more traditional "right hand" of the golfer. But there are still some golf courses that require the use of the more conventional method—a personal caddy.

When a golfer plays on a course where a caddy is required he or she is required to pay the caddy for the progression of the golf course. Carrying the bag is a physical benefit to the focused golfer, but this is not the only purpose and function of a caddy. In fact, the caddy's job is a multifaceted craft. The caddy is often called upon to know the details of the course, such as knowing the correct yardage for each hole, the layout of the green, and the way the weather conditions may affect play. Ideally, the caddy should also be attentive to the player's style and individual abilities. An experienced caddy can offer correct advice on what are the best options for the situation at hand. A good caddy is also responsible for providing oftentimes-necessary emotional guidance to the player in order for the person to function at the top of his or her game. In essence, the caddy becomes the advisor and counselor to the golfer during the course of play.

On the fourteenth hole Easter Sunday at the 2004 Masters, Phil Mickelson faced a difficult shot to the back pin. According to Mickelson, his first inclination was to hit the ball in low, but Jim Mackay, his caddy, suggested he throw the ball up high and let it bounce back to the hole. Jim was right, and so Mickelson nailed it. He went on to birdie that hole which was one of many outstanding shots that gave him the momentum to go on and win the Masters.

If you are a serious golfer you could increase your score if you had access to a good caddy. You need one you can trust and who could offer guidance and assistance at crucial points of the game. There are many professional golfers who do not feel comfortable playing without their regular "man on the bag." The reason for this is that the longer a caddy works with a specific golfer, the caddy becomes more familiar with the respective abilities of the player. Essentially, this allows the caddy the adeptness necessary to offer sound advice and consultation to the person.

No doubt, if a new caddy is used each time a person visits a golf course, the consultation will differ because of the unfamiliarity in the relationship between the golfer and caddy. Therefore, the success rate will be inconsistent. In effect, the better and longer standing the relationship is between the golfer and the caddy, the more precise and effective the guidance will be to the golfer.

The Christian and the Caddy

So far, we have determined that the responsibilities of a caddy include the following: carrying the heavy bag of clubs, being familiar with the details and layout of the course, understanding the skill level and individual abilities of the player, and offering counsel, advice, and encouragement to the player as needed. Remarkably, all Christians have been provided with their very own personal caddy to walk with them day in and day out for the rest of their lives. That caddy is the Holy Spirit.

Jesus promised His disciples that the Holy Spirit would come and teach them, guide them and instruct them in all things. "But the Helper, the Holy Spirit, whom the Father will send in My name, He will teach you all things…" (John 14:26). "However, when He, the Spirit of truth, has come, He will guide you into all truth; for He will not speak on His own authority, but whatever

He hears He will speak; and He will tell you things to come" (John 16:13). The Holy Spirit is continually available to the Christian who is walking the course that God has destined him or her to walk.

Letting Go of Your Bags

It is so easy in today's world to become burdened down with the cares and frustrations of daily life. These day-to-day things can oftentimes become heavy loads that we carry around with us causing us to feel tired, weak, discouraged, and vulnerable. Jesus taught His followers that when this happens we find rest by releasing our cares to Him. "'Come to Me, all you who labor and are heavy laden, and I will give you rest. Take My yoke upon you and learn from Me, for I am gentle and lowly in heart, and you will find rest for your souls. For My yoke is easy and My burden is light'" (Matthew 11:28-30). The Holy Spirit is present with us to take the load off of us so that we can focus our energy on finishing the course that has been placed before us. The Holy Spirit carries our bags for us and supplies for us the tools and advice that we need in order to successfully finish our course in the strength that He provides.

Even though you may find yourself walking unfamiliar spiritual terrain, the Holy Spirit, being the perfect Caddy that He is, has already been there. He has gone before you and has become familiar with the road you are walking. He knows where all of the hazards are, He knows the best way to reach the goal, and He knows what tools you will need in order to get there. You will never find yourself walking a path that the Holy Spirit is unfamiliar with. He will be an expert Advisor and will see you through to the end. Regardless of the severity of the situation you may find yourself in, the scriptures teach us that He is capable of guiding your footsteps.

> …He leads me in the paths of righteousness for His name's sake. Psalm 23:3

> In all your ways acknowledge Him, And He shall direct your paths. Proverbs 3:6

> The steps of a good man are ordered by the Lord… Psalm 37:23

> For the Lord knows the way of the righteous, but the way of the ungodly shall perish. Psalm 1:6

> ...The Lord of hosts, who is wonderful in counsel and excellent in guidance. Isaiah 28:29

Since, the Holy Spirit is guiding your footsteps and knows the path you are walking, you can be sure that as you listen to His advice you will successfully complete the course and advance to the next level spiritually. The Holy Spirit is your professional Caddy and He is always with you, guiding you every step of the way.

Knowing Your Skill Level

Most caddies know what the players are capable of doing on the golf course better than the players themselves. It is no different with the Holy Spirit. He is a keen observer and knows how you handle yourself in the midst of challenging circumstances, chaos, trouble, and trial. He knows you better than you know yourself. He knows your strengths and your weaknesses. In the book of Revelation, He said to ALL seven churches, "I know your works..." (Revelation 2:2,9,13,19; 3:1,8,15). He followed up with listing the positive attributes and then the negative ones. He knows what you are capable of and if you are willing to listen to His voice and heed His instruction. If you listen and obey, then you will be able to refine your skills causing your character to be molded and formed into an image that is pleasing in His sight.

As the relationship between the caddy and the golfer grows, the golfer begins to rely more heavily on the advice given by the caddy. It is no different in the Christian walk. Anytime you find yourself in a situation that you are confused about and do not know what to do, then you can turn to the Holy Spirit and ask for help. He will offer you counsel and advice to see you through the trying times of your life. The Holy Spirit is always present with you. He is always there to teach, guide, and direct your steps as you progress on the path of destiny the Father has placed you on.

Chapter 8
Securing a Mulligan

Golfers go to great lengths to play, but no man has gone farther than Alan Shepard who walked on the moon in 1971. Ten years after he became the first American in space, Shepard gave new meaning to the phrase, "Shoot for the moon." He stashed a Wilson Staff 6-iron club head and two balls in a tube sock he had hidden in his spacesuit. After Apollo 14 reached the moon, Shepard snapped the head onto a 33-inch aluminum rod used to collect soil samples. "In my left hand I have a little white pellet familiar to millions of Americans," the astronaut told the world before dropping a ball on the sandy lunar surface. "I'm going to try a little sand-trap shot." Hindered by his bulky space suit, he made three one-handed swipes—wiff, chunk, shank. Frustrated with the outer space limitations Shepard decided to take a "mulligan." With the help from a lunar gravitational pull only one-sixth that of Earth's, he cranked one 300 yards, with a 35 second hang time.

What an example of taking golf to a new level. But even on the moon Shepard needed a mulligan. It has happened to every golfer at least once—the desperate desire for a second chance. It is what we call a "do-over" or a "mulligan." Imagine the sound of your club cracking the ball and you hear the velocity of the ball whistling in the wind only to see it take a nosedive like a kamikaze plane in World War II into the pond before you. Your friends laugh aloud and snort at your shot. When that good shot became a horrible shot, you could sigh a breath of relief. Why? Because you can call out, "Mulligan!" and do it over again.

The opportunity to use a mulligan is not an official rule of golf; in fact, it violates the written rules of polished golf. A professional golfer like Tiger Woods would not be permitted to use a mulligan in a tournament. However, most "weekend warriors," including myself, use them religiously when a drive, a putt, or a chip is unacceptable.

The exact origin of the term *mulligan* is uncertain, however many golf club resorts claim to have had a member with the Scottish/Irish last name of Mulligan who would frequently allow himself a second shot on a bad tee. Eventually, the term Mulligan became common practice in friendly golf circles. Other legends state that some bars and saloons had a free bottle of alcohol called a mulligan. Somehow the term crossed over to refer to a "freebie" swing in golf. Whatever the origin of the term may be, many golfers are happy to accept and utilize the mulligan when they make a dreadfully atrocious shot.

Do You Need a Mulligan?

When golfing the feeling you get when you drive your ball into the trees or the water is pure misery. Many times your buddies in your four-some will act like Job's friends—at first it starts modestly—then turns to sarcasm. One of them will get started and the other two quickly join in making fun of your calamity shot. If you are not careful, your failure will affect your game.

There are going to be times in your Christian walk when you will make a wrong turn, a bad decision, or just frankly mess up. The Bible says that sin is "missing the mark." It is when you aim for the fairway and you end up out of bounds. When you sin (hit a bad shot) you can go to God and ask Him to forgive you. He will restore you and give you a second chance. All you have to do is ask and God will pull out another ball, drop it down and give you another swing. This is the beautiful thing about having accepted the Lord Jesus Christ. God is a God of the limitless mulligan. "If we confess our sins, He is faithful and just to forgive us our sins and cleanse us from all unrighteousness" (I John 1:9).

The good thing about a mulligan is that you don't have to stay in the sand, the water, or the woods. When you request the use of a mulligan, the ball is dropped in the middle of the fairway where you originally hit your ball. You get a fresh shot. If you find yourself caught in a hazard, you don't have to stay and fight your way out. Same thing with God. All you have to do is ask your Father for a mulligan and then pull out a fresh ball on the same spot where you had previously made an error.

Hitting the ball off course can cost you dearly. Nothing can be worse than hitting a great distance shot only to sink it into a sandy bunker. Many people dislike playing from a bunker, especially a fairway bunker. As you try to dig your way out, you can't help remembering that it was an awful shot that got you there in the first place. While pros make it look it easy, it is a grueling challenge for most amateurs to hit the ball cleanly and judge how far it will go.

When you do end up in a sand pit, there are just two options. One, you can ask for God's strength and wisdom to learn how to get out of the mess you're in. Facing the reality of the fairway bunkers can be a potent reminder of just how comfortable it is to play in the fairway. But, occasionally, we all need that reminder. Learning to play from the bunkers can also help us play better from the preferred lie in the fairway. But the second option is for you to ask God for a mulligan. Then God's grace can sweep in and give you another chance.

Life teaches us a similar lesson. The "bunkers" of life are inevitable. We might as well accept the fact that hardships come to everyone. But before you find yourself in one of life's "bunkers," it is best to learn how to get out! Complaining and moaning will not help. We must face the fact that we are off course and decide the only way out is up.

God wants you to have another shot at life. He is not mad at you. He wants you to have another chance to get everything right in your life. I want to pray for you now:

Father, I lift up every man and woman reading these words. I pray that you will reach into their hearts and help them have a new beginning in life. There are some that because of broken relationships they feel like their lives are ruined. There are others who feel they cannot reach their goals because of finances, job situations, or past failures. But God, you are the God of not only the second chance, but also the third, fourth, fifth, sixth, and seventh chances. I ask you right now to give them a new start. Give them a mulligan, Lord, so that they can begin fresh with you. In Jesus name, amen.

If you prayed that prayer with me then I want you to know that God is working with you and is in control of your life. You have no need to be worried. He is giving you another opportunity to get everything right in your life. Remember, He is the God of unlimited mulligans. Any time you feel as though you've made a bad shot, just call out to Him and He will give you another chance.